If I Could Work

Text copyright © 1987 by Terence Blacker

Illustrations copyright © 1987 by Chris Winn

First published in England by Walker Books Ltd, London

For information address J.B. Lippincott Junior Books,
10 East 53rd Street, New York, N.Y. 10022.
Printed and bound by L.E.G.O., Vicenza, Italy
10 9 8 7 6 5 4 3 2 1
First American Edition

Library of Congress Cataloging-in-Publication Data
Blacker, Terence.
    If I could work.

    Summary: A child fantasizes about the different kinds
of work he would do if he weren't so young.
    1. Occupations—Juvenile literature. 2. Work—
Juvenile literature. [1. Occupations] I. Winn, Chris,
ill. II. Title.
HF5381.2.B55 1988   331.7'02   87-3972
ISBN 0-397-32245-3
ISBN 0-397-32255-0 (lib. bdg.)

IF I COULD WORK

WRITTEN BY
Terence Blacker

ILLUSTRATED BY
Chris Winn

J. B. Lippincott   New York

If I could work instead of play,
I'd get up early every day.

I'd drive a bus and shout, "Fares, please!"

I'd rescue cats
from the tops of trees.

I'd be an inventor and make lots of toys,

I'd play the guitar and make too much noise.

I'd be the world's
favorite TV star,

I'd be a doctor and
make children say, "Aaaah."

I'd open a shop
with sweets on the shelf,
When no one was looking
I'd eat them myself.

I'd smile at people
as they drove past,

I'd stop them if
they went too fast.

I'd be an incredibly silly clown,
I'd make people laugh
when my trousers fell down.

I'd be the first child
to go to the moon,
I'd tell my parents
I'd be back soon.

And I'd fly back home
at the end of the day,

I'd really much rather
work than play.